Laundromats & Lounges

ROGER SMITH

Copyright © 2013 Roger Smith

All rights reserved.

ISBN: 978-1484182116
ISBN-13: 1484182111

DEDICATION

This book of poetry is dedicated to my heartbeat, my wife Joy-Anne who always believed that my words were more than just my mind peddling through the crackerjack box of vocabulary, but they indeed are the prize one searches for. You are the epitome of love, blessings, and pure excellence. It is through you that I am certain God has major favor upon my life. You are my strength, my weakness, and every emotion in between. Thank you for always being supportive of my dream, and helping me to realize it. I love you. It is also dedicated to my three inspirations from heaven, Trinity Aniyah, Tarynn Aliyah, and Teyana Amiyah, to further show them whether you're awake or asleep, your dreams never die, and with God in your life, even if they fade, they can be brought into fruition and rejoiced. I take pride in having three beautiful, God loving daughters. I would do anything in the world to ensure you each continue to be filled with happiness and individuality. I am extremely proud of all of you. I love you and will continue to do so unconditionally, until the day I die.

CONTENTS

Laundromats & Lounges	1
Reflections From Poverty's Balcony	4
Knowing Love	5
I'm Not Ready	7
Man-Made	10
Everglades	11
High Chances of Precipitation	12
Pyramids	13
Mask of Amerikkka	15
Edit the Truth	17
Away With Anything	19
Regurgitations of Disease	21
Checking Character	23
Upon Building My Thesis	25
Drunk Off Collins	26
Scribes & Scriptures	27
the Inner Beast	28
I Too, Have Dream Variations	30
Trema Orientalis (Charcoal Tree)	31
Across the World of Classrooms	33
Intimacy Lost Between Garlic Sauce & a Slanted Gaze	35
Blend of Dos Mundos	36
Dichotomy	38
Heartbeat	39
There's an Invisible Barrier	42
Evenings in Her Orchard	45
Recognizing Genetic Inheritance	46
The Fibers of My Soul	49
Emphasis of Desire at 4 am	51
The Architect's Destruction	52
Reconsecration in the Midst of Emotional Chaos	55
Means to an End	57
Lies & Matrimony	58
Thoughts of a Predator	60
Staircases of Affairs	62
The Cycle of Man	64

The Numbness	66
Silhouettes & High Heels	68
That Night in July, 1970something	69
The Cirque Di My Soul'e	71
EBT's & Ramen Noodles	73
Still Not Televised	74
Media is Like An Abortion Clinic	77
Catastrophes Definition	80
History & Darkness	82
Dim Bulbs, Highlighting a Year	86
Friday Nights & DVRs	89
Half Cracked, Fully Shattered	91
Emocean (ih-moh-shuhn)	92
Transcendence	93
Etches of Life's Tomb	94

INTRODUCTION

Laundromats and lounges. One place you travel to and commit yourself to the labors of cleansing, not only clothes, but ones character. Here the washing of one's thoughts ensues and we continue the series of events that coincide with a Laundromat. We rinse the rage of our days while the spin cycles of all of our lives simultaneously run, but no two are in the exact same position. As large as the world/Laundromat may be, we're all one on top of the next going through the daily activities of survival, dampening us, weighing us down, and soaking others in painful experiences as we all look towards The Lord to dry our souls through hope, faith, and perseverance.

The other place people go to unwind and forget about all that eats at them. Listen to a little music, relax, kick back and enjoy this life before it's all over. The conjunction and, merely tells the story that they work in unison with each other. If you're working, and trying to clean your mental state you have to have somewhere you can escape all the ills of the world. My walk with God has drawn me close enough to Him, that he is with me in times I face the roughest spin cycles of life. He dries me off quickly and has also become my lounge. The Most High is my area of escaping the nonsense surrounding me. He slips into my soul and stirs my creative juices and gives me a serene calming to face another harsh sequence through the tumultuous turns we face in this gift called life. Some of these poems were written before I was reborn in the blood of Jesus as a Seventh Day Adventist, so I pray you enjoy walking with me in my journey becoming the man I am today through many of my Laundromats and Lounges. God Bless.

LAUNDROMATS & LOUNGES

ACKNOWLEDGMENTS

This book could not be complete without the following acknowledgments, the people who kept me afloat all of these tumultuous years in the rough seas of life. To my mother Vernese, and father Albert, for life, love, and instilling the seeds of ambition and creativity within me and keeping me always on the right path. To my brothers Ronnie and Craig for love, support, and keeping me grounded at all times in every endeavor. To Cerlene, Omar, and Tori for guidance, and the help teaching me patience, perseverance, and acceptance (plus all of the Sabbath laughs). To the greatest team on Earth, my extended family: Brian Tulloch, George Walton, Millison Thenor, my sister Kenya Bey, Karla James, Lori, Charisse, & Brenden Sobers, Roderick Burnett, Shawna Murray, Keith, Kevin and Keren Davy, The Mingos, Kevin and Sabrina Perrin, Fadisha Richardson, Stephanie Smith, Jaxon Brown and family, Jamaal Smiley, Tom Perri, Lutando Hamilton, Andre Talbot, Marcus Simmons, Isis Petrie, Mark Anthony & Maurice Hunter, thank you. To my aunts, uncles, older cousins who helped raise me, everyone in my family, my in-laws, as well as my friends and co-workers, (especially my Service Execution family and Valerie Ware) for continually holding me down and raising me up; know that you have played a pinnacle role in my growth and development into the poet, man, father, son, brother, friend, and confidant that I am today. A special acknowledgment to Joseph Chilman, English professor at Molloy College, for urging my exposure to more poetry which consequentially has broadened my horizons and helped me become a better creative writer. God Bless you all.

"An artist must be free to choose what he does, certainly, but he must also never be afraid to do what he might choose." – Langston Hughes

LAUNDROMATS & LOUNGES

Laundromats & Lounges

there's a lounge in queens village called the pour house,
you'd be wise not to ask for a shot of prosperity.

i ordered a glass of hope,
topped off with bitter dreams
shot down by crooked cops
and sirens sang
from their stools.

put a quarter in the jukebox,
if you dare
listen,
the nine to five men
struggling to pay their bills,
the everyday house wife needing a sip of something
just to deal with her kids,
the middle class; classless,
suffering from summer's dry, thick, humidity,
bank accounts like mouths,
thirsty.

the bartender's eyes are no more filled
with poverty than a newborn.
her smile whispered
brightness, that this merely part-time,
night-time oblivion,
though day time academics couldn't have taught her anointed head
and hands,
to tap
dance over beer mugs overflowing,
surely goodness and mercy
shall follow her, all the days
she communicates with consumers
of her art and craft.
she speaks eloquently
even through vodka induced, liver weakened
stress fractured ear drums.

in the air lingers the smell of fish-
net stockings chased with torn,

worn out latex mixed
in a familiar stench.

tomorrow's sorrow
holds hands with the infantile reality of today,
and springboards
into snifter
with aspirations of drowning in cognac.

the bar itself,
is a bloodstained, vomit infused cherry wood,
with tips
plastered all over it.
dime sacks, nickel bags, copperheads
and tales of how not to end up here,
in the back,
where pre-Magellan's flat
Earth lies;
with sticks, balls, holes;
traps
for uneducated balls to roll into,
moors to fall into.
into an abyss which hovers over
ground so close to home,
the familiarity
crowds the entrance;

blocks away
the exact same people
exit
a Laundromat,
carrying wet clothes, loads,

and pockets quarter filled with
quarters quarter
filled with lint
half empty but fully conscious
of clean, dirty and indifferent
they,

like the fabric
are survivors of the tsunami

they,

pour experiences into
wash, rinse, and spin cycles
to increase the resistance of letting tears or sweat fade
origin of character
they,

cover frail feelings with rigid skin snuggled with fabric,
softener;
and this juxtapose is
just supposed to be ignored,
but it's Wednesday.
drying clothes or buying a metrocard, is a
decision left to ponder
two days before payday;

next round on me.

Reflections From Poverty's Balcony

No doors, no walls, no structure.
You call it a home,
But it's our world I refer to,
And stomach growls and hunger pangs concur
With words I construct
While looking into the dam like eyelids,
Of fresh outta womb pre-grave orphans,
Offering themselves as entertainment
For the scraps you've tossed away for the past three weeks.
The weak and the meek intertwined,
And though God promises they will inherit the Earth
Their worth withers
Like kitten's carcass whiskers
While we,
Don't give, don't offer, don't notice
Their existence
Or, the Baseball bats swinging home run like yells for help at us
And tattooed S.O.S. on our foreheads
While their community takes communion with cemeteries' residency...

We see them as refugees as lost souls,
But they build on experience's tragedy
Like the re-creation of Babylon from the rubble of recluse
And in turn See us as outcasts,
as black sheep, as the ones who in Actuality–
need help.

Knowing Love

like children dancing on the playground,
the Earth spins
His universe, her galaxy, our world
within its own cipher
turns hand over hand,
overhand and underhand
like the twisting of braids and locs,
spinning through the
evolution of boy to man, daughter to mother. son to moonlight
shedding light on the one constant:
His atria, her ventricles, our love.
our minutes and hours spent, as buildings crumbled, walls fell,
the foundation of devotion,
stretched its
limbs beyond the limits of sentiments,
withstanding trials and tribulations
pulling like loose strands
of hair,
fused like dreads sent from heaven,
and the heaven we know, of wrapping arms around
one another as everything around us
turns like hands turning
the ropes of double dutch.
we clutch voices, hearts and hands in a remarkable forever,
embedded in an eternal union of you and i,
yet i never knew love until i held my child…
from womb to infant
in an instant, my anatomy tingled with excitement of ooooh!
i can't wait til the mornings i have to do her hair
that i can't,
and ponytails, pigtails, will all look like oxtails,
as i look like the donkey…
and overprotective of daddy's angels, of daddy's little girls
of boy you better not call my house
so late,
and lately it's over joyous tendencies of them telling me
what they did in school,
and daddy can i have this,
and daddy oooh i want that,
and daddy, daddy, daddy-

and the word daddy grabs me
as water filled my mouth, nose, eyes, and ears for a few seconds,
and cleansed mind, body, and soul,
the word father
was no longer synonymous with belt, backside and discipline…
palms touching, no longer had my mind rolling
like the twisting of new growth,
bended knee was no longer followed by proposals,
stomach growling continued
before being silenced,
and walking in the footsteps of humility,
had nothing to do with what was on my feet.
i now concentrate on the ultimate sacrifice,
of not giving up one's life,
but giving one's life as He, gave his for all of ours…
said i look right to my wife,
and left into my children's' eyes,
but i didn't know love,
until i found Christ.

I'm Not Ready

we never played catch.
but i attribute these words
to feelings u instilled in me.
from liquor to love,
discipline to slinging
diction,
praying for the weak while
preying on the weak
minded.
procreating, i recreated a family with values
you valued, and i am
so proud to be your son. like
as the sunlight shines,
the darkness inside of me fades
because i'm growing in the midst
of the lessons you learned me.
and though i teach
your granddaughters, and we, pass a bajan-american heritage
thru the hills,
my mind still focuses
on you.
blood pressure medication to the top
of the bottle,
cap popped off mount gay rum
in cups catching
mouthfuls of beer,
and swishing thru, gushing to kidneys
flushing you, while
liver weakening,
while weakening
the very source that beats within me.
how could you not tell me
you were "going home to die"?
and the water running from my eyes
sprints to desktops
as i mask my pain in noise, in love, in everything
you taught me to mask my
genetics in,
fight hard. drink hard. love hard.
and i, punch drunk love

without Sandler's stupidity,
God damn you
never, played catch with me.
and i'm remembering
every six love shared as the dominoes
fall in my mind.
knocking down blocked memories,
of beatings
kids who behaved badly got,
that i hated but loved as i got older.
recognizing
each lash was outta love
and kept me outta cells, and selling the illegalities
of the substance
you infused me with.
you yelled words of protection.
you cussed emotions to make me a shell of rigidity.
you hit me with man preparation hands,
and thick skin
wraps thick skull
and causes me to breathe thick air, into
thick lungs unclogged,
cause you kept me away from cigarettes
but blew a heavy smoke in my mind,
and in my heart,
yet you've come to a decision.
a peace, a serenity
of leaving me without giving me my rightful goodbye.
though you never threw me a ball,
never taught me how to swing a bat,
you are the homerun of my life,
and you didn't
even tell me you were ready to leave the ballpark.
i can't get out the inning
pops.
no outs. bases loaded and you, nor anyone else didn't
prepare me for this,
you never taught me to swim, and i'm
drowning in my thoughts.
outlets of love, can't understand the thoughts of this man
cause i don't understand,
a thought process you proceeded to procure,

and pen of mind is scribbling but, i can't finish
these thoughts, for when the period falls
maybe so does this thought...
and i will never stop thinking about the possibilities that,
you might take your last breath
and left me,
millions of miles away dreading it,
dead within
and while i think cries
the ink dries,
my eyes prepare for the worse,
seeing you
knowing i froze when i should've told you, i love you—
yet the same eyes prepare for alleviation,
seeing you in my soul.
seeing you in my daughter.
seeing you in every thought, every action, everything i have become is a reflection
of not, what we haven't done,
but what you've made me.

Man-Made

Fathered,
Thus I must accept the term man made.

I have kissed more lips
Than cared to recall and left
The lingering stench of a poet:
Love, liquor and bullshit.

Fingerprints imprinted on paper mate thighs, and glitter
cast away on the shores of my pubic hair. I dream in off pink sunsets,
where lip gloss peels like paint chips
on shaft walls.
Picnics with private parts on the menu, I've laid, on man-made blankets
staring at clouds of ballerinas,
spinning on an axis
almost as if spinning off acid,
sipping pink beer through a straw.
I have shot, lilac-tipped bullets
at rapists, pedophiles, and queers
then rode off into purple mountains
on unicorns screaming
Yeeeee-haa!
I carve love letters and 7 line sonnets
into myocardial muscle with crash carts chained to flowered tanks.
Ignoring tears,
I have the emotions of Ken
though more flexible at the joints.
I have never had a happy thought,
nor do I understand
rainbows, ponies or perfumed infused
sodomy disguised as aromatherapy.

The thesaurus doesn't link
fear with love, I am man-made,
I have no sons.

Everglades

it was like staring at an immaculate
portrait of
the epitome of winter.
frost, sparkled on the head of
princess, like
snow on the Everglades. fancy dress
covered her like bark,
the air, cold.
the crowd, speechless
as they breathed in
her glacial artistry of tiny twigs
squalling
in a typhoon of elegance in a Brooklyn ballroom. her branches
balanced beauty
and bravery beyond words, as
she soaked up the sunshine smiles
from all in awe,
except the empty seat where the planter of her seed
should have been.
in disappointment, she twisted twig
and it snapped.
tears ran down her petite trunk,
but water can't heal her, though she'll continue
to grow from this experience,
her future as the dancing tree
is over. she'll be uprooted,
and replaced
in the Spring.

High Chances of Precipitation

Beauty shouldn't require a raincoat,
and yours, of complexity
which would launch a thousand ships,
shouldn't have so many streams
and as dream catchers try to catch you,
cousin of Cleopatra,
daughter of Nefertiti
descendant of Isis,
mother to Theresa, my atria coddles you;
ventricles cater to your needs,
valves shut.
detouring disappointing deliberations
of past
actions that only existed
in cerebellum's screenplay,
which starred constellations created
by ardor's concept construct,
and conceptions so immaculate
Testaments testifying against it,
would be drowned,
rather baptized in the bayou of your beauty.
our bedroom is Sierra Leone and your eyes,
your eyes are blood diamonds.
Your stare crucifies.
Guesses exhaled, breathe inhalations of reassurance
as pulse idles.
Clear!
your kiss resurrects,
only to have me floating yet in your allure,
Osiris never needed an umbrella,
why the hell should love?

Pyramids

The sands, storm around the base,
spinning around solid foundation as we, watch in amazement
questioning the conception
of a structure created by the
Omnipotent hands of God, gazing at Giza,
staring into the sun shining on the back
of the pyramids.

Definitive, undeniable shape of heaven crafted,
towering over me I bare witness to the Nile
acting as umbilical cord, nourishing earlier civilizations
as legendary futures, become historical pasts.
Grains of sand enter my nasal cavity and I breathe
in the essence of life, tasting millions of years
which have the calculated scent of a few trimesters.

Positioned next to sisters and protected by
the guardian Sphinx who flanks the temple,
rather the body...
The perfect portrait of a pyramidion,
less material high with a majority of weight pushing down
towards canals distant from Suez's,
anatomically
built of Nubian limestone labeled melanin.
I see cultivation within angular eyes
and the rising population of pharaohs, in wombs
of Egyptian ancestry.

Images depict you,
wonder of the world.
Wondering how you stand strong for lifetimes, as
time gives life before you,
while nations disrespect you,
wild masons abuse your meaning
taking you for granted, when they should worship
the sands beneath,
because you, silently screamed in childbirth as the Sahara
deserted you, just as the Blue deserted him before,
and the sand storm cycle continues,

blowing the genetics of fury through the placenta, to be washed away in the Red Sea,
but it's not.
It travels from dynasty to dynasty,
through your heartbeat in Cairo to that of your offspring in Aswan,
creating sharper edges,
strengthening your stone-like exterior
from apex to base,
every face of you is exquisite.
Your goodbye causes the sun to set
and I've finally learned to say I love you in Arabic,
black mother to be you are,
a pyramid.

Mask of Amerikkka

i lay in pain
counting sheep,
as they put another brother to sleep.
no pillow, no blanket
no country tis'ing of thee.
no liberty, no freedom. just injustices middle finger.
another whisper
of 'nigger', from the crowd.
another time, the system we're supposed to trust in,
showed us how disgusting
it is,
with injections less lethal
than the nothingness proved
by unreasonable doubt,
rather, invisible fact
that you're guilty once you're black.
and we sing, songs of cringing
while thinking of
abner louima, and amadou diallo, and sean bell, and jena six, and darryl hunt
for the less known,
pragmatics which set the standard for
snooze button like reminders that,
this is not our nation,
though we built it.
this is not our government, though we voted one of 'us', in the top spot.
and while we hop scotch
through life, dodging bullets, slurs, and inequality
which leave us maimed all the same,
NEWSFLASH,
the Civil Rights fight ain't finished,
just the movement.
so start moving, stop stagnating a nation of young, inexperienced
Kings and Princes,
who don't know fights past King, cause that's all the system teaches.
passive aggression,
but the time for diplomacy is done!
this nation has slaughtered thousands of Iraqis, they called it War.
ten-thousands of Indians, they called it Discovery.
hundred-thousands of Africans, they called it Progression.

Millions of Black-Americans, yet Refuse, to call it Genocide.
still,
purple mountains majesty,
scream Murder.
ring Murder.
vote Murder.
Vote, Murderers!

Edit the Truth

you could walk around,
up, and down
the aisles of Barnes & Nobles,
with a smile all noble
laughing,
but i hope you ain't laughing at me,
cuz i don't wanna be,
"that kinda poet".

i want my pen to be as free as my speech,
breaking the barriers, you set.
i refuse to be a sellout,
oh no!
my trees are far too personal, to smooth over,
and while i move over to the other side
of literature,
stand there, in the aisle emotionless.
look through the titles,
realizing
the category of poetry, not poet-trees
is lacking. lacking that seed of inspiration,
twigs of creative juice like sap
seeping into the very crevices
of brain matter
which gathers a thought of motivation in young readers
and writers alike. Hmph!
you can read those other half fulfilling laureates,
but i betcha
their words won't get under your skin and open your veins,
and allow that blood to rush,
or hold still your heart. oh, no sweetener to stir you eh?
nothing to make you question your beliefs, your visions, your
imagination.
you can have your three piece suits and ties,
your crack white cash, your Nobel prize.
you can keep your awards, receptions, your full course meals,
your sold out events, your publishing deal.
i didn't want this talent in the first place,
but since i have it,
i'll save face,

and replace books and pages
with phrases
that'll amaze, political characters
and poet actors.
no you won't see
this collection nor the next in stores soon,
cause you don't want me to get into the minds of
the youth,
you don't want me to be a best seller, a household name,
or a textbook sayin',
you want me
to simply,
edit the truth.

Away With Anything

rivers are liars
rivers run away
away with emotions
away when you need
need is a fallacy
need shatters dreams
dreams get misplaced
dreams crushed by life
life is a setup
life battles failure
failure is a river
failure tricks men
men run
men misspell love
love like lust
love whispers to women
women desire rivers
women bathe in deceit
deceit ticks on wrists
deceit thrives on time
time is up
time is invisible
invisible like love
invisible like forever
forever laughs
forever outlives death
death is a motherfucker
death denies hope
hope sleeps with dreams
hope is blackness
blackness is power
blackness creates beauty
beauty of sex
beauty is broken pencils
pencils sketch rivers
pencils breathe poets
poets are liars
poets wish
wish for greatness
wish to die

die young
die happy
happy to love
happy to be
be something
be anything
anything that ends
anything but poetry
poetry
ends.

Regurgitations of Disease

There's a disease within me.
it's not affecting my
ability to write,
to love,
to think,
but it's there. And
as i awaken from lymphoma's coma,
i witness, all
the reasons i'm fighting for a life
worth living.
i'm envisioning every purpose
God gave, miniature doses
of diagnoses early.
i'm laying in a painless pain—
with dry eyes crying.
meanwhile, cells metastasize inside
via
venous highways, arteriole parkways
and capillary drive,
thriving on a life driven by wisdom
and beautiful children.
i sit,
embodying anti-life antibodies,
that various biopsies
brought to optics reality, that there is
a therapy, within
the disease within me.
and as radiation
radiates to my soul,
i think i'm losing control like the Hulk,
but these ain't gamma rays
Gran Gran.
i find myself talking with dead relatives,
trying to relate to a life
i use to ridicule,
cause of stress that seems so miniscule
to my many, mini views
of my own "We Real Cool",
and then, the buts, and what ifs? return to my thought process,
of losing this gift

of literature, along with this gift
of breath, giving to him thru her,
the eyes of a queen, staring into
love which can only
focus on the disease.
the disease that left my mind to think about it,
that left my heart to love without it,
and took shape
within my body.

Checking Character

I walked up to two homosexuals and told them,
I don't understand you...
I don't understand how you'd rather hands like mine,
mixed in with lies, chauvinist behaviour, and canine characteristics. get how you'd rather rude
dudes with physical
strong hands,
bowling boulders, building buildings,
rather than,
drink milk from where you were born, and told her just the opposite.
to drink milk from
supple breasts of the moon
which birthed stars,
constellations straight and
bent with purpose,
giving light to pitch black sky, but your
focused on the bulge in my pants,
and told her just the opposite.
the sweet must, of jockstraps
and hairy testicles
colliding with the antichrist comfort of your goatee, and
all of Massachusetts cheering
you on in a half sense of relief for freedom of choice,
half sense of fear for their sons,
singing songs of anal rape and sodomy,
fear their wedding gowns
will collect cobwebs for the rest of eternity,
fear that virginity lost,
will be lyrics of vaginas French kissing
at the Louvre
or worst in Greenwich Village, fear
that penis will replace
thermometers taking temperature,
axillary, orally, anally, but,
of adolescent boys
who are not in catholic school,
who never dreamt of going to the
State Penn or Penn State
for that matter. I
asked him what it is about size 12 feet

caressing his legs under
300 count threaded sheets,
asked her what it is about sipping
from the sippy cup of the
God given birth canal,
asked him why he wishes to
swish semen in his mouth and
grunt, snore, belch, and fart
in masculine unison,
asked her why she needs to have
four nipples, two uteruses,
multiple eggs dislodging, flowing
all month into Always and
ten personalities under the same roof,
and they both looked
at each other, looked
at my hand, locked eyes on my wedding
band and said to me,
married men seldom understand love.

Upon Building My Thesis

Every lecture you listen,
never walking out. Never
excusing yourself to silently snore,
as people who never held scalpel
(yet are educated enough to be called doctors)
dissect my brain with rambling wrath of report,
to be regurgitated
at random moments,
as are names of Ground Zero's casualty,
still, years after. My thoughts,
tower.
My mouth. My pen. Like twins,
drop,
as if Hypnos took rest on my eyelids,
you,
don't budge.
Like gunshots screaming through the air ripping teenage flesh in
East New York,
whiteboards wince at markers edge.
Blackboards, cringe at chalk
like victims of rape in Central Park,
and echoes,
and echoes,
and echoes that I envy you,
empty seat in Kellenberg.

Drunk Off Collins

before I married poetry
I held it up to the light,
as checking currency for the invisi-strip, then turned it off

then pressed so close that it tickled my auditory nerve,
my last, in which poets get on.

I dropped a roach into the lines of loose leaf and flicked the light of a poem
on and watched, thoughts scatter while dreams sneak into fruition.

I crawled inside a poems' tomb
and felt more life
than in drama's delivery room.

I zip lined through the rain forests of a poem, drenching the right lobe of
my brain, soaked and nourished from outcasts
scribbling similarities of the strife of poetry.

you, still insist on imprisoning
laureates in prerequisites,
crucifying the contributors of creativity,
impounding arts' immortality,

and continue to strike words with hoses,
dissect ink
and search for the etymology of a poem.
I will tamper not, neither shall you with my cocktail of inspiration.

Scribes & Scripture

I've laughed at comedies and
cried at tragedies in Elizabethan,
Victorian and all sorts of English,
Un-English to an English major.

I've read poems of battles and voyages
longer than novels, histories
and odysseys between
pages of ingenious, intellect and indifference.

Poets have asked me about dreams differed,
authors of raisins in the sun and I've contrast the two
as I've watched mine go up in smoke
from relinquishing grip on bic.

I've studied stories. Stories
shorter than my children, written by
who They, taught me were legend,
of men, mice and mockingbirds.

I've put my ear to floor boards
as if they were seashells, listening
for heartbeats because of reading,
comparing tales of
New York and Los Angeles with
machines un-timed,
un-matched, un-equal,
but still considered good quality scribes.

I've read plays
during the recess of my life and
essays while sweat worked its way
down my brow on those twelve hour shifts; shifting memories
to articles of war on drugs, war on terror,
war on the middle class, war on education,
war on war like war,
was on steroids and raging
as someone whispered what it was good for,
absolutely nothing.

Newspapers have crossed my eyes path
with headlines of crooked officers,
getting into the Guinness Book of Records
for shots fired. Man down as shots fired at unarmed men murdered,
while mothers mourned
their children lost like paradise.

I've read pro-black, pro-white
and cards in crayon
as powerful as documents
from Massa breaking the bonds of slavery,
declaring independence to independents,
and
allowing me to vote.
Thank you.

I've read those that have no words written
like smirks, smiles
and seduction.

I've read hundreds of
laureates,
dead, breathing, and alive,
but the one that will stay embedded
in my Richter scale of progression,
in the land of all literature read,
was written by a white boy on the walls at Rutgers University,
and read,

Niggers Go Home...

the Inner Beast

what comes to your mind when you think of black?
do you think
of chains,
cages,
and enraged slaves
battling for the rights
birthed to them,
fighting for freedom their ancestors
before yours earned for them.
does your mind ponder
notions of moses
being black...
do you think of pioneers,
or apes,
a system twisting us into their visions
of monkeys running
through the wildlife of Afrika,
banshees calling us brothers,
us in rectangular cages
with arangatang faces.
is that depicted
in the unwritten diaspora of blacks...
do you witness greasy hands
banging drums,
beating ghetto noises
at decibels too loud for european cars,
and can you hear those
loud, cuss words
disturbing neighbors,
next to your neighborhood,
from hoodlums
with tropical fruit stained lips.
is that what you feel
when you close your eyes
and think of black,
or are your eyes closed every day.

I Too, Have Dream Variations

looks like that white day won't be done,
still, for you
i sling my arms wide
in the center of the sun...
resting from dusk til dawn,
beneath a tree
bout to fall,
i notice my dreams
ending, short never tall.
nightfall, almost over
though still dark, like us.
my dream of billions of blacks in unity,
not millions marching
so get on the bus.
focusing on my dream
i too Dance! Whirl! Whirl!
when i open my eyes
at gunpoint, my heart curls,
mainframe wrinkles
and blood boils,
to see a shadow of myself, behind
the gun. my dream now,
a pure toil.
as daybreaks,
my dream does too,
my last thoughts are "Dream Variations",
inspired
by you.
so look down with dejection
as the gun shot heard from Harlem to Joplin,
and the fall of the tree,
as my dream was stolen
by someone Dark like Me.

Trema Orientalis (Charcoal Tree)

Footstep after footstep
through the tumultuous turf,
the clanking
rejuvenates the anger. The wind
blows; ashes, dust and, leafs flee limbs
making space as do
passengers with similac dreams for baby Parks.
And even before that time
we lingered in the balance of oak. I,
am staring at the world's oldest
charm bracelet,
thinking of how her kiss, decimates charcoal.

How does one pick her flesh in the sunlight,
caress it in the shadows,
and have nightmares of it, while whip whistles, whirring
lashes of love and whispering passion to prisoners
both pre, and post
persecution. She cries for me,
and it's these tears
which will puddle beneath
my resting tree, but all that matters is
her kiss that decimates charcoal.

No grave, no
tombstone. Just coarse corpse,
next to decaying mulatto
infant, ripped and
wrapped in umbilical rape claimed claims. No pillows
to rest my head,
like upon her cloud like appearance. No
apologies
for thrusts of payback sex acts,
for secretive teachings of readings,
for late night watering which grew
hidden devotion.
Just the divide of humanity and
reminiscence of those lips,
which decimate charcoal.

Love has me lifted,
swaying from side to side
on its arms stretched out;
Out-stretched past the cotton fields in the sky.
I've survived all my days
feet planted in dirt,
though I hadn't lived until
her cotton candied lips decimated my
charcoal, this moment
is a testimony our love is real.
Don't you ever let 'em cut me down,
from her kiss,
off her lips,
i'm hung up.

Across The World of Classrooms

She glanced once.
And her smile ignited my insides,
Damn... i'm gonna owe Con-ed,
Cause there is an electricity between gazes which amazes blocks
In cities named Watts when I witness this.
She makes my soul shine,
And sends my mind into overdrive running red lights, signs of stop, hazard and yield,
School crossing and deer crossing the same,
and I'm talking bout the fact, that she, merely facially frisbee'd me,
a smile.
An involuntary action of corners of lips yawning, moving just to keep loose, or
stretching to give nose high fives.
A mere exercise building muscle structure for lip locking activities later with
thoughts that, there has to be a Mr. Wonderful in her realm.
But here in mine, she blinks,
As to conceal the marbles of her soul.
Her smile, again says hello to me
Just as her hips do.
Wondrous waves
Swaying parallel to passion,
Perpendicular to the pleasures of my mind,
Her skin looks as if my ancestors picked it themselves, to hold for that one
who they'd last imagined,
As they dangled from southern oaks.
Her complexion, is a mixture of rejuvenation with shades of jubilee and
undertones of heaven
Surrounding her mouth.
She speaks, and at start I cannot hear her due to amazement that divinity
parts.
Then as the DIRECTV of my brain searches for signals
I tune in... Tune into the mp3 of Matthew whispering to Jesus, her voice
echoes harps, violins, and violas,
As the orchestra of her words
Bounce around the stadium seating of my skull.
My nostrils breathe her in,
but it's too much.
I take her in, but can't hide that I'm taken, and the tides
Too much for me to bear.

I was barely there, but her waves have me a cast away;
A class away from being comfortable
In another class,
Maybe I would be.
If this were Myth and Legend, I'd be Poseidon.
Instead, she performs, and I'm a child.
I am flounder swimming around chasing her words with auditory arrthymias, following
Her next thought like Simon says.
She, is the little mermaid.
Her waters are still,
Calm,
Unlike the very feeling she brings about within me.
Within the seas of my veins, there's a crashing into lighthouses, flashing my arteries, my capillaries and flooding my heart.
I am falling, for the figment of my imagination.
We are simply lovers in a glance,
Class mates sharing air
But not breathing the oxygen which mates our souls,
So I continue,
Continue scribing poetic hieroglyphics of a modern day Cleopatra,
And she continues pining my soul with a face sketched with a calligraphy pen handled by Leonardo Di Vinci,
inspired
By the Holy Spirit.
I am in awe.
Admiration and inspiration
Scream silently like green lights in cardiac rush hour traffic,
crushed... I look off,
She frowns.

Intimacy Lost Between Garlic Sauce & a Slanted Gaze

If only eyes were cars
(they'd be more than windows)
now
vehicles to the soul and
she, would turn on windshield wipers
of delicate Hyundai,
as lotus flowers and jasmine gust through the air
of Confucius Plaza.
Soft hands that once massaged
toil and turmoil
into pleasure and content,
now serve
as shield. For her,
tears are disrespectful daggers,
launched at dragons
by samurai during battle,
not passion. Frenzies, of yearning and fury followed as proverbial
chopsticks fed on the innocence
of geisha to be. We part lips of yin
and yang,
to conclude the dynasty whispered between
pillowcases filled of
Hennessey and opium sweat,
chased with the aromatic scent of cherry blossoms.
The slants of traffic
now overloaded with whitecaps
remind me of stories I heard my grandfather speak of:
the chopper lifting for the final time,
as he gazes into the headlights of
the village girls
his platoon ravaged, with love-
hate pelvic thrusts.
I stand in failed attempts, forcing heart to skip a beat again,
just to convince myself
the situations differ, though she
quietly turns away
with white rice boxed tight emotions,
she murmured in a breath of bitter ginger,
"sayonara."

Blend of Dos Mundos

Subliminally,
she screamed instructions
to keep her young, stir
her creative juices with the sucré of my words,
just add water. Salivary
glands jumped at the chance
to change glance into stares
on the staircase of friendly faces;
subtle smile,
luscious lips,
and an anatomy wrapped in nationality
outlined in a strategic intrigue,
shadowed by a simple sexy.
From a distance, she yelled whispers
of galletas y crema,
between labio and labia,
overstuffed Oreos are crushed
under
four hundred count threaded sheets
leaving crumbs of passion
and a half full glass of 2% milk
chased with intimacy we,
protected our hearts like El Morro,
Brooklyn Bridged our loins, and
sketched portraits of the Empire State Building in San Salvador
on cerebral canvases.
Paper,
would allow me to kiss la perla del Sur,
in return, siphoning my
manhood with each stroke she etched.
Without speaking, she asked me to kiss her privately. Not in her private
place, but her face said otherwise than body led.
I fed on the fruits of her tree
and gave life to sin that would shame Eve. She sucked,
with lips of inspiration
y una boca of both
sexuality and excitement. She
was always never everywhere
but crept into vision, somewhere

the silent superstar
finally gives me an autograph
scripted in Spanish,
but spoken in a language foreign to
both of us.
she poses nude behind a closed door,
and I touch myself in my sleep,
while dreaming of
chicken wings y habichuelas,
a blend of two worlds.

Dichotomy

Eight letters. Three words. Three, syllabic structures
you
could've uttered
at any given moment but you,
wasted the ticking of the clocks' hours,
like men in charge of powerful nations
un-united at round tables, arm wrestling
over nukes and resources while lives
are lost; minutes
like broken condoms shellacked in baby oil,
semen and spermicide; seconds
filling up the engineless humvee with
no wheels,
no ways to get around,
no steering,
GPS-less and clasped to the emotions of the pump;
no, I don't forgive you
Fuck your flatline--
I hate you!

Heartbeat

"when I get that feeling, I want"—
More healing than sexual
seductions can provide
from twin tower length legs
and thighs,
leading to perfection of visioning
Caribbean sunset eyes,
and the sound in between of her,
telling me,
she
(Lub dub. Lub dub. Lub dub...) Me.

I need, intellectual
conversations stimulating
possibilities, of raising trigonometry infants, inspired by
true change, not just vocals behind a podium.
I need lips, whispering subconscious subtleties,
of foundations unsinkable
in this relations-ship, as we sail
thru hail storms called poverty,
hurricanes like unemployment,
and any other disaster on the rough seas of my
(Lub dub, lub dub, lub dub...)

It's not enough to just spread the North tower from the South.
I want to intertwine our lives together forever
like dreadlocked run on sentences,
menacing one another's tomorrows with subjects
and predicates, of many moments of mini intimacies
and, conjunctions of her days with my nights
with, propositions and proposals
mixed into pictures, framed around a picketed fence palace, she rambles
about
at a table playing bridge with wrinkled ex-pageant runner ups.

"I said when I get that feeling, I want"
Warm, polar bear hugs,
and spooning which makes utensils cringe.
And carry me, when I'm unable to carry her, as she carries my last name, no
hyphen—

I want Coretta while, I have a dream
and the pillow is still crisp,
as I sleep walk thru a 12 step program, from addiction to kisses,
conversations, and constant smiley face texts
while we, l-o-l in reality without TV.
I'm sorry Marvin,
but I wanna drive thru every one of her 365's.
cruising the highways of richer or poorer,
swerving on the interstate of better or worse,
speeding past sickness and in health,
not just park within her and get my ticket validated.
I want the valedictorian of the class of women
cut-
ting sex ed. to be next to me, in chemistry.
proud of her man,
holding hands
humming Pomp and Circumstances...
Glancing at ring, illuminating digit on left side of hand, of our globe
spinning, into a combining galaxy, in a closed room
clothed,
while womb waits...
I wanna hear the preacher man preach his, "dearly beloveds, we are
gathered here" to hear my now
(Lub dub lub dub lub...)

But that's not cold feet, that's the warmth of reality, the excitement of
companionship,
the Super Bowl winning catch
the landing after jumping the broom,
the biggest, loser, winning.
the result of fighting against all odds to see anniversaries unseen by
too many divorcees,
filing at your local supermarket in aisle 13,
but that ain't for me.
I don't want 15 minutes of sexual healing.
I want the feeling, of feeling,
Extraordinary!
Of being superhuman. Of looking into her eyes, and seeing me as,
Immortal!
When "I" get that feeling,
I visit her gravesite, and flood the soil
reminiscing of her,

Lub - dub, lub - dub, lub - dub,
my one, true, eternal

There's an Invisible Barrier

There's an invisible barrier
in a marriage,
subtle transparent walls
tapped by concupiscent urges. Urges of
I miss you talk
and long walks, through dark parks,
and pass strange folk, with neither smirk,
nor smile loaded faces. Faces loaded
with confusion and chaos
such as their nine to five lives,
worries of child and pet
like conjunctions of puppy chow
and grilled cheese.

This barrier is engaged as soon as
you're pronounced,
man and wife, husband and woman,
dumb, and dumber, respectively.
We search for something
in someone that we don't think
exists within ourselves,
because it,
like that barrier, is invisible. Invisible like
fear, like love, like God.
Three things that
march left foot, after right foot after
cold feet together,
down
that aisle like marital militia,
in expectance to go to war.

Expectance that her chambers will not
always get along with
your cranium, and the systems involved
will begin a bar brawl,
because usually, alcohol tends to
shorten the barrier height.
And without short talks,
her smirk leaps through dark parts

to slap smile off of your
face. Slap, loaded with chaos and confused
thoughts that she, is strange folk
walking in circles
because she, can't get through the invisible barrier and
she, is aggravated that your being
offered meow mix and grilled steak
as a night cap, to nourish
concupiscent urges
that you, don't want anyone to fill,
lustful itches
that requires no other nails to scratch,
keyboard love punches
typed only by,
the one on the other side of that
transparent wall.

A wall you're
not responsible for,
but take all the blame as if you
shellacked the Sheetrock,
spackled holes of :
what's for dinner? who are you on the phone with? why is she going out
again? are you drunk? whose earring is this? you don't need new golf clubs!
how many pairs of boots or shoes or high heels can you where at once?
and painted over all of that with,
I love yous. I miss yous. its okay,
but that's not the case.

You both
walk,
holding hands, carrying insecurities between them like
palms of magnet and metal
out of that initial park, through dark tunnels,
imprisoned in
emotional tunnel vision systems
called marriage,
putting on subtle smile
to confuse that smirk of chaos.
You engage in a strange unusual
game of chess,
like children, chasing each other around

your daytime, intermediate, graveyard shifts,
like playful
pets, carnivores, cannibals.
Each others face,
an invisible barrier.

Evenings in Her Orchard

Eyes of mahogany that catches me.
I am Bambi, and cannot move. Movements
like ballerina slash gymnast, slash
runway model,
modeling of the latest designer flesh,
she waves hands.
Each finger a wand of its own
working magic and mojo, her voodoo
intensifies affinity.
Highway thighs
which lead to, and fro passions capital
with no speed limit posted.
I am often pulled over.
Under Courvoisier toned complexion,
I sip from her bosom, and
take shots from her lips,
welcoming her toxins to run as O negative rivers within.

Without thought mighty serpent,
I take the same path again!

Core. Seeds. Sauce. Juice.
I full guts with the epitome of thee, oh apple of my eye,
if eternal life lingers between
her kiss and the abyss of humanity
then I'd gladly answer to the name of
Adam.

Recognizing Genetic Inheritance

You should be ashamed, of yourself.
Mahogany mannequin,
mascara doesn't make you up,
it merely distorts
the portrait he perfected,
while you portray to be lighter, to be darker, to be taller, to be shorter
and shortly you
won't depict graphics designed by his eye, I
should be ashamed.
Of words that speak
catastrophes blasphemy, as the guy in that looking glass,
looks passed
chisel brown beauty in which was held,
and handcrafted by the potter,
and I don't mean harry,
had he
wanted me to look like Denzel, I would. You should,
be ashamed. Of aching feet complaints
cause when legs were restrained by grapples of the world,
you were carried.
Carried through despair, dejection, dishonor, degradation and the deepest
sin
yet still,
you weren't dethroned, dismissed, or desanctified, in his eyes, I
should be more than ashamed.
Of actions acted,
when dirt, soil, dust or land
touches hand.
That which touches body which he, created us from
as I was sculpted with rocks of every emotion
and impacted with protection from my imperfections,
every divot
replenished by the gospel.
Every digit, to do his work as an apostle,
but my man-made mind pauses, like semi-colons, commas and apostrophes,
I'm possibly
just as simple minded as my ancestor Adam.
And, as we try and add him
as a Facebook friend

we fail to realize that He is within,
every step,
every breath,
at every time, every chance you glance
in that mirror
and doubt… whatever it is you doubt,
you should be ashamed.
That you don't witness this, prediction of
Head, cerebrum, cerebellum, medulla, and stem
that guides all, thinks and analyzes the love given
and not Tail,
slithering on belly
hidden in grass, gravel and lurking. Nor the insight
that you are Above,
the enemy tugging at your feet, collar, shirt
skirts, coattails and inner animosity and not
Beneath, like the lava boiling in our
blood with anger, hatred, envy, jealousy
where Lucifer lays watching.
Because you don't recognize the divinity in being a
Lender not Borrower, but constantly indebted
with credit and debit debts,
of unpaid, unsanctified, unnecessary
so called necessities
to drive fancy what. He has golden chariots awaiting us.
Big mansion where, here?
Forget reality's mirage.
I should be ashamed,
of fooling you thinking these words
that clutches the curves of your minds speedway are mine,
so find your highways, running parallel with his byways,
and disregard this
indirect detour,
cause right now we're speeding backwards in neutral,
and his plan is not to place blame
but to show the shame of this mere man ,
so you can share as
we. We
should be ashamed.
That we don't cherish his pointed pencils
which etch our sunset for sunrays to soften our given gift of skin,
or that Christian chalk that sketches

borrowed winter breath of life,
the permanent pen that scribes our name in the book of his glory, grace and his will,
still,
why do we so often ignore the reflection of our inheritance,
the photograph of his Kingdom to Come,
the camera phone illustrations
of His.
We should be ashamed, because He told us
we were created in his image
but seldom
do our lives reflect, pictures of prophecy.

The Fibers of My Soul

when you're down,
hands down
i'm man down,
but when u smile,
you ignite the epitome of inspiration
within the creases of the beast;
and when you kiss me,
i'm simply embracing the lips of an angel,
and understand
the significance of God's love
the bond of two beings
seeing each other through
ups, downs
and the inevitables of existence.
when you cry ,
i wade in the waters of humanity,
and would drown
in your sorrows to save you from them;
but when you laugh,
heaven opens up
and i begin listening, to the harps of your heart,
the violins of your vessels
and the drumbeat that unites our affection,
the warmth of not just
a woman,
but the woman of my nocturnal sleep,
the woman that King dreamed
dreams of,
that Luther sang of,
and that Martin jokes to hear
speak voice. voice of
sweet sounding Barbados
crashing against the todays, tomorrows,
and the forevers
of my world. a
world which exists to keep you in it,
a world which renders me helpless without
visions of
birthed princess, angel and blessing
that you have blessed me with.

when you weep, in wanderings of why,
you withhold the wonders
of what the Most High
embedded
in brown skin, dread,
bottling up nurse, mother, wife,
beauty itself at its finest;
but when you love
like you love me,
the Lord, adores the world that took Christ,
and cries nothing but hope.
if our daughters
evolve, into half of what you are;
(you,
the immaculate love structure,
you,
my devotion to oxygen.
you,
the absolute joy of my breath,
you,
the hidden piece, completing the perfect puzzle,
you,
above anything, my all),
then we,
have produced gems of pure paradise.

Emphasis of Desire at 4 am

Uninvited, though not denied i sipped the nectar of my queen.
Pillows arched her back as hips unlocked and expanded.
The blanket shadowed my heads rhythm as she awoke to realities dream
of clenched fists full of sheets, and every desire her body demanded.

Frustrations, built up like eleven story buildings my loins began to growl
from a yearning that ached. A pining, of steady engorgements below
seeming to stretch seven of the longest days, as i await her anatomy to howl
in languished ecstasy. Finally, her fluids of felicity have freedom to flow.

Her inner thighs grasp, caress, and kiss my earlobes with force,
as fingers comb uncombable locs, etching passion in my scalp as they crawl
through. She delights in mouth's autobahn designed course
which races against climax as tongue drives and crashes against wall.

There is no pit stop on the track of orgasm by oral orifices this sweet,
no better way to assassinate desire, than like a silenced colt, under sheets.

The Architect's Destruction

i am, i
am feeling minuscule.
mind half the word,
swimming in an ocean of emotions
yet drowning in my own thoughts,
caught off guard by
Gods calling,
yet the phone never rang.
busy signals keep me busy,
mean whilst
flat lines and dial tones
intertwine like the fine fibers
of my hair,
locking reality with my fears
and there she is.

i woke up to the Lord crying at my window
angels shrieking
at the keeping of a soul taken too young,
someone
save me from mental incarceration,
spiritual imprisonment,
and cardiac confinement,
because blinding visions of ribbons in the sky
slowly tell me the good,
die
younger than they should,
and my heart weighs a ton
as the keyboard
loses function from desk puddles,
cheeks turn soggy
from rivers cried,
and nothing, nothing bridges this pain with understanding.
even though Mama said there would
be days like this,
father never said when they'd cease,
and pieces of peace,
are no closer than the light at the end of tunnel
which is probably

a deceitful glistening, of teary eye
listening to
sullen atria, pumping love throughout my soul.
i am sullen. i'm sullen and cold,
dismal days turn to nervous nights,
and fright renders
my hugs on my little ones, into chokeholds,
away from
going back to the essence,
and since this incident,
i question my sins' innocence,
and the bitterness
makes me experience a doubt of
rationales existence.
all of this fuels the fire of waking up, pissed off
cause we are pissed on,
which leads me to just losing more water,
yet my daughter's words echo
in the emptiness of my mind,
"Life is fair, because we get to live",
but she never said how long…
but this seven year old who taught me this,
never whispered
kisses of how long will we have to witness,
witness this fairness
of this fairy tale shit.
so my fears, are increased by three, and divided by a wife
i can't live without,
and while now doubting my bond with, Our Father,
has me bothered,
for if he calls them
i will break every bit of the fragment
Graham Bell invented,
and vent a ferocious yelp
that texting Yele won't help,
and these thoughts within me
sends
walls smashing in,
brainwaves and mainframes crashing again,
this notion,
is my implosion.
and the blueprints imprinted in

my lifetime,
didn't have hidden structures built for protection,
so everything
falls upon my mind, my body
and weighs heavy on
me…
oh my soul.

Reconsecration in the Midst of Emotional Chaos

As our lips touched, our mouths opened and love
entered my soul. The combination of two worlds,
Venus and Saturn. Intrigued by my rings,
she created an instant self hatred.
Intrigued by her lips, my blood boiled for a kiss
and wouldn't simmer until ours clutched.

She, listening to the resistance within, clutched
her heart and hid it in the shadows of love.
In her neocortex and thalamus, we kiss
at short rapid instances but long enough for our worlds
to conjoin and expand into a hatred
for the illumination of symbolic rings.

I, stand in a stupor, until the phone rings,
now caller id has heart clutched
as I answer, and she says, "Hello", with no hatred
in her voice, just love,
and it settles the quakes and waters of our worlds.
She tells me her mind still lingers on the kiss

that has body calling for another kiss,
that has soul, desiring rings
for herself, to legitimize a union of worlds
other than genitalia clutched,
other than the mere act of making love.
My silence, stirred the hatred.

A rebuttal of anti-sentimental words of hatred
and regrets of partaking in kiss,
in partaking in lust delusions of love,
neglecting rings,
and further ignoring screams my heart, already clutched
could never maintain residence of shared worlds.

Tears, sniffles, and anger signified the separation of worlds,
signifies the sporadic growth of hatred
in seconds. One misunderstands the clutched,
unlatched attachments of a man's kiss,
the interest deceased, once recommitted to rings

meaning, and the initial vow to love.

All the world's a stage in which hatred
is developed by loose rings and an insignificant kiss.
The result is usually disbelief in love that keeps many a heart clutched.

Means to an End (In the Rough)

Pressure.
the clouds, skies, and atmosphere
wear down on weary shoulders,
which carry things heavier than mountains
like,
responsibility.
Cutting wrong like knifes
I stop my bleeding,
her sweat,
their tears,
all equally polluted like the Hudson.
My soul,
like my soles worn, from walking for us during marathons for cancer called
love,
I stare into agnatic irises
knowing the unknown is worth
every breath I take and lose,
every smile from
my chambers quartet,
is a diamond.

Lies & Matrimony

how could you take that ring,
how could you, betray this thing.
this thing of ours,
of, intertwining souls,
words and passion.
i, was so used to our bodies
bonding
like the strands of my hair.
i was so, used to
nourishing my needs
from your wants.
i, was so used to thinking
that,
your decision to keep a little me in your womb,
would soon
string us together
like violins of ghetto intimacy,
orchestrating
your thighs, around my waist,
of hatred
wasting away,
creating a combination
of beautiful oxymoron
like, seductive adultery,
as i savagely sip
from your sweet poison.
away, from the realities
of love at first bite, i run through
recollections of
first sight of you,
in your poetic goddess-ness, and
how you introduced yourself to Satan
as Aphrodite,
and your lips ripped through flesh
as they mouthed hello.
how could you take his name,
and all that
goes with it.
avoid my lyrics,

and destroy my spirit
all with the forever echoing "I Do",
when deep within
you do not, cannot, and will not
faithfully be his misses,
when you, are undoubtedly
mine.
so says your mind, heart, and spine,
night after night
your voice whispers
sweet kisses
of love thought lust,
combusting what you are leaving of a man,
barely breathing,
now, loins bereaving
the passing of our unity,
the back turned
on love, locked and dreaded
now, i dread the vision
of you next,
with finger hugging jewelry,
named changed,
game changed.
but will your eyes still play the same?
and as u whisper
"i do",
i too,
die within.

Thoughts of a Predator

i felt her within my spirit,
luscious lips whispering kisses that this would be
different, yet it never is. And
as blood rushes past pulses,
thoughts of getting it in, has
me settling,
as money and world exchanges
i walk thru, settle in, then
i let her in
subtly, then suddenly she attacked.
Back, bruised from nails
which rip into part of me, letting
punch, drunk,
sweaty sex love acrylic,
slip into arteries,
leading to teeth, sinking into
flesh torn neck, bone,
hambone, hambone have u heard;
the words of anatomy's tragedy.
As her hands ran down
my abdomen, the pull of gravity,
pulls shaft, while
pushing the shrieks of my soul further
and further, behind
the Yeses from my voice box,
and the ice box
turned on.
Frozen atria and ventricles of tundra
held tears back, and screams under
lip biting, writhing
as genital fighting began, she ran,
heels up my hamstring.
While mistrusting thrusting took all of me within
her, strumming my pain with her fingers,
lust lingered, and
for every minute we shared our most intimate vices,
of our intricate devices,
although the passion was priceless,
orgasms couldn't suffice with brainwaves wiping out

the hearts surfboard.
No one heard my soul yell
Cowabunga Dude!
Rude tongue, wrestled the aggressive walls of
her wet womb,
our creams of life, intertwined in the most beautiful hatred ever created,
and i controlled her body's banshee-esque bellows,
like a sexual Geppetto,
yet the strings of her hearts harp
sounded more like footsteps, and while i faded into nocturnal heaven
she closed the room door and unplugged, thus
severing our connection.
And it starts again, the nothingness of the game,
the shame that i can't
formulate her name,
yet the emptiness is the same. Damn,
my mind can't understand that
there's no morning after pill for a man.

Staircases of Affairs

I
Man meets lady, met
by unexpected tingles.
Blood plus moisture flows.

II
Uncontrollably,
she smiles and licks her lips.
Intrigue bursts within.

III
Like a woman, she,
blinded by necessity
ignores golden band.

IV
First date, leads to first
kiss leads to many pleasures.
Caution less, she falls.

V
Constant talk of work,
days are wasted though nights are
spent full of recess.

VI
She whispers, "I love
you" who walks out without pause
and never gazed back.

VII
The bulb has broken.
Pieces of glass, scattered next
to pregnancy tests.

VIII
After the month you
let pass. She calls to inform
you of life's changes.

IX
Vulgarities lead
the conversation with no
warning or warrant.

X
I'm with family.
My wife, my two kids. A new
never mentioned world.

XI
We swapped juices.
The intimacy held God's
attention not mines.

XII
The incisions of
words, ripped every part of heart.
Outside must match too.

XIII
A visit from her
sister was the only way
her cold corpse was found.

The Cycle of Man

"Don't wanna play no games I want you exclusive".
and as i think of her,
my butter brown sugar, sweetening
the very air i inhale,
i realize there is no more juice
pouring out the fruit
of my main squeeze,
so i— exhale breaths of a side piece,
while focused on breasts on the side,
and peace hasn't played a role
since the towers crumbled...

that was us, standing tall by one another,
redesigning the alignment
of a skyline God envisioned when he molded
the first architect,
out of mud and marble,
and as we quarreled about blinds, placemats, and room colors,
we were
blind to the placement of each other,
that if we looked thru the eye of loves needle,
the color of any room is passion red,
which blooms
to hues of baby blue,
but instead baby boo, you chose to neglect
my emotional needs,
physical wants,
and my mental desires, which turned made me
interior re-decorate
mind and body,
with soul of a side piece.

And pieces of my soul
sought spiritual guidance,
but no counselors were able to council, and conceal
the scent
of her happiness from my words,
the essence of her smile in my eyes,
the slight shift,

her fingerprints left in my chest.
she consoled my past while catering to my future,
and presently she's pregnant,
not with child
but the offspring sprung off from my creativity.
I've planted the seed of words
within her womb,
and she has sucked grammar
from my eight and half by eleven inches
and swallowed my distinctive ink.
that jealous tingling,
is only an inkling of how,
pussy and prose be
mingling in poetic states of passion.

I walked up and down the aisles
from marriage to Macy's
and left with the fashion of a side piece,
besides
fastening a piss poor pass,
I stitched lips to your ass for too long!
became a boy scout to learn
various knots,
as not to grind the ties that bind.
I find that redefining openings will lead to better closure,
rather than bitter exposure and bullshit, petty beef,
but you, tried to unzip a button fly with your teeth,
and no tooth fairy
can put us back under the pillow, under the sheets, under the same roof,
looking up at the same ceilings, laying in the same bed,
cause I lay on my side at peace,
with my side piece,
peacefully whispering...
"Don't wanna play no games I want you exclusive."

The Numbness

i remember when my chest cavity
pushed ribs in expansion,
as if heart was digitized to explode upon her presence,
and mind would be ready to implode,
with brainwaves activity being active with premonitions of her hand
running the 800 meter across my back.
back in a time when I'd read smoke signals
that people on wall street couldn't make off,
instead were Bernie Madoff'd, and in order to see them jump to their demise,
I'd have to look down,
cuz i was floating on cloud nine,
off recollections being bambi-ized by headlights of her souuuullltrain,
rather staring down the green miles hallway of her eyes
not knowing tomorrow, yesterday, today
nor the difference between the three, cuz the two of us, were one with zero doubt.
i remember the hula hoops in my stomach,
abdominal excitement writhing
of, uncrunched sensations;
nooks, crannies, and creeks which obliques couldn't understand,
but i had it as she entered the room
like i'm back in 3rd grade and that ooooohhh!!! i didn't do my homework
feeling took over.
reminiscence of our palms, making love as we
walked with them braided into the next
and wedding bands like rubber bands
played as berets,
while anxiety, nervous-relaxedness and passion greased the scalp
of a union to be never divided.
i remember kissing the dotted line of finding forever between
her bloodstream, and her voice.
the closest thing my auditory canals could imagine an angel's harp,
strumming my words like R.Flack, and aflac
can't provide supplemental medical for myocardial infarctions,
sparking fractions of half, can't bring back full-time
life and for the life of me, i can't remember the action or fight which
pinched last nerve
and brought on this internal numbness.

a numbness, that i don't cringe when she cries,
i don't smile when she laughs,
or turn my head when she enters the neighborhood.
a numbness,
that makes me hold my breath when she exhales as not to poison
my inner cells,
as world hears couple, yet we see cellmates.
the warden said, "death of jealousy in a man is progress",
and i've heard a correction officer say "nothing lasts forever",
and a foolish inmate's rebuttal was "what about love?"
what about, four random letters in the alphabet,
a tandem, like word peddling
tantrums of emotion which becomes as faded as the memory
of my first steps,
her first bottle of milk,
your first giggle, or the first slap of the same babies belief
that they no longer feel,
and in this instant the whines and (baby cries)
return me to similarities of things long gone.
it's not about whether or not you get your heartbroken,
the frightening inquisition is,
whether or not you'll even feel it,
do you feel it?

the abominable layers built around atria and ventricle
spreading iced plasma to extremities,
frozen swollen opened tear ducts,
duct taped integrity
telling me i feel nothing- nothing.
"sssshhhh"
says the numbness.

Silhouettes & High Heels

Jaws
jack-hammering stage, spewing
marble, pheromones and green dyed worth-less
wood chip ligaments which independence's
father imprints. Eye in
awe,
incarcerated by socket
cornea angers, pupil stretches, duct sweats
at thoughts daughters' thighs
mask truth,
hypnotize masculinity with affection disguised,
and siphons testosterone, and wallets like
pythons do her
prey...
for mothers with mammary Himalayas and debt to match,
silhouettes and high heels; thin
inhaled, smoke infused, aphrodisiac engaged
Ear,
listening while breathing while moving
with tuition driven
actions, flashing cameras under lights.
Mind speeds past traffic traps in arteries and veins on
son's anatomy,
engorging the essence of gender identity,
mouthed lullabies from Lips that house lies, which boost blood pressure,
heart rate and ego,
she witnesses this...
against the artist within,
the child who dreamt of Rembrandt,
who paints images of seduction on mental canvasses.
airbrushed lust stroked assets, her Hips sway,
her love sponge, drips paint thinner,
The Night Watch
stripped.

That Night in July, 1970something

I remember visions of nothing,
and nothing but darkness
surrounded my eyes like a raccoon
in a strange environment.
She, with light brown windows to an honest soul,
stared into the black, oblivion of mine,
and told me
to be still and keep quiet,
as she constantly ordered me. She
kissed me and told me she loved me,
but not like she kissed him.

Without speaking her body played
rhythmic arrangements
of Cupid's arrow in B Flat. Like a lion
in the wild, he fed on her, she
was his prey and he ravaged her as
such. He erupted molten of vulgarities
as if her name didn't exist to him, while
she dug,
as if digging for my grave site,
red, nail polished daggers of passion into his back,
fingertips pleading for more,
while simultaneously screaming
for a God
she never believed in.

As the king of the jungle let loose his
roar, I heard zipper rise with
the faint flick, flick, flickering
of lighter. As the slim foreshadowing
of cancer grasped her lying lips,
the flame allowed disappointing hazel
to reunite with resenting blackness
of mine. In a disgusting relief
his pocket regurgitated rent,
lunch,
and cab fare to get to work
tomorrow night.

As he left, he turned, threw her a quarter and said "get a soda pop for
the kid." A dim hotel
light, illuminated the entire world
that night, as I watched
the conception of my bastard brother
from behind a broken, battered closet
door,
which led to mini nightmares,
and many nights paying psychologist's
student loans,
wondering why every relationship
I get into, ends
as a short stay.

The Cirque Di My Soul'e

I creep in, smiling contagious.
Left dimple the measles,
Right dimple the mumps,
she calls me a clown.
Frowning is not a function
installed on my network I, am ecchymotic soul,
rhythm and black and blues
She says no! I am red nose and big shoes.
She, says I cram words,
nouns, describing verbs and action less adjectives into mini cooper verses,
structured fiat stanzas
and demand laughter at every (water sprouting flower into eyes) moment.
Eyes which watch a destiny,
envision visions which reveled revelations,
and rebelled emancipations proclaimed by, white face, red lips and concrete
smile. She,
often judges like Judy, like Maybelline
making up my world as she goes along dancing in her ring of three.
Her spirit, untamed like the tigers of the wild.
Her mind, more contortionist than her body as if it shifts from lover,
to mother, to maid, and this made
her optics, sharper than blades cutting thru box,
with person and mirrors hidden.
Splitting anatomy in sections,
her breasts are rings of fire,
intriguing to the eye, yet hot to the touch, but no one is ever ignited. Her
thighs are elephant trunks, long, thick, and nourish her in their entirety. Her
lips the trapeze,
sending men flipping,
keeping others upside down,
holding on for dear life her vagina is the tight wire.
Wired tight for balance purposes, yet everyone's walking all over it! Yet,
she's pissed off cause of my big shoes and red nose.
Yes I'm a clown,
My smirk, is a 70 inch Samsung, not even standard, but low definition.
My smile, a three year old throwing temper tantrums in public libraries
during a moment of silence for fallen heroes.
My laugh, a four hour long emergency broadcast signal in digital Dolby
surround sound.

My chuckle, crickets behind the bedroom wall, which awake only when it's
time for you to sleep.
She, remains in her jigsaw shattered remains of a residence,
pulling stones from her high horse,
rocks from her pedestal,
bricks from her comfort zone. I,
infesting the air with tuberculosis cheeks, walk out.

EBTs & Ramen Noodles

i stood on Murdock in a hoodie tasting the rainbow.
i stood on Murdock in a hoodie tasting the rainbow that
ends in no pot of gold, just lint and
dead white men printed on
dyed paper,
falling into society's new fad
I'm looking both ways.
I'm looking both ways
for dollar vans that cost more than a dollar,
while teenage Cleopatra
trade royalty and crown for
title match
between chicken and pigeon while
their language,
language that breaks champagne bottles across ship and sends young men
to war,
language that chases witnesses from front door like loose pit bulls,
language, sandwiched between stench and vomit, smeared in feces
that she heard, now she hears,
that subconsciously makes me revert to my childhood and,
tuck my blackness away,
while simultaneously checking the sag of my denim. Her eyes scolded me,
Too Late!
I am slave chained and hand cuffed
to her prejudice prisons of
bodegas and slang,
hip hop, aspirations of basketball diaries,
all she sees is,
EBTs and Ramen Noodles.

Still Not Televised

the revolution,
will still not be televised
because there will be no revolution.
and dreams foreseen,
have turned into mere men, with visions
settling to slide pass the system,
and our words are all we have.
so poets, write.
singers, sing.
and rappers, chase millions and lead children
to early grave yards, while preachers,
preach and false teach
to get into little boys pants,
and dance illegal and ungodly
while others write, for a revolution
carved in the skin of Nelson Mandela.
bleed for the journey home
that Garvey inspired,
while so called brothers,
sling white rocks
and sacrifice their sisters
to white folk.
though all cash is green, the faces
on them smirk.
old blue eyes. not the man with the golden arm, but
white faces whispering to each other,
the revolution
will still, not be televised because the revolution,
has been put on the back burner,
and we've turned to acceptance,
rather than rage
and pages of our history, constantly
jump, rather leapfrog
                                off
pages enslaved, and cage us in,
raping us of happiness
and while turning from Christian,
to Islam, to Rastafarian,
GOD, ALLAH, JAH

or whosoever you choose to call the almighty
can't feel we,
and mentally, i'm crucified.
brothers disdain and pain,
mistake my soul for Medgar and
drag me,
like February 21st 1965,
when the space
between W and Y was erased
from this place. poets, scribe daydreams to escape the reality
that rapid protection shots from policemen
shred flesh like Kraft sharp cheddar,
grating hearts, and thoughts
go back to CNN spokesmen
yelling, the revolution will still not be televised
because there will be no revolution.
and shootings
turn into everyday happenings,
and our children have no sense of who they are,
and slavery, transcended
to mental slavery
so now abolitionists
pick up pens
and bleed unto pads, then bleed unto paper,
and bleed unto ears, through mics
to rewrite constitutions in Braille
cause we are blind. and
visions of 1865s
ratification seem less evident,
but we bypass, expecting
to be basketball players no, football players, what about baseball players,
now even golf stars,
ooohh the next tennis legend,
when the only athletics we used to dream of,
was the 10 yard dash from watchdogs.
my brothers still know about
the 100 meter dash from badge holders
and street patrollers,
but we buy into this raising our kids like
zombies leading them to sports rather than books,
when all we have is our words,
words which read: the revolution will still not be

televised,
because the revolution is yesterdays talk.
ku klux klansmen
at the million man march wouldn't
even be noticed
because we're more focused on Jay Z and Nas having "beef",
than swastikas still appearing.
and though our eyes still tear from
slashes on back,
scars embedded in mind,
and ancestors flesh burning from whips and chains,
the youth yearn for fancy whips and platinum chains,
and plantations turn to penitentiaries
turn to, graveyards
with tombstones reading the revolution will still not be televised,
cause like a reality TV show,
all we would do
is WATCH.

Media is Like an Abortion Clinic

the media is like an abortion clinic.
can you hear it?
can you? do you fear it.
the media, is like a poets abortion clinic
slowly killing my spirit,
pointing fingers
in directions
undirected.
blaming black directors for movies,
black artists for songs,
black authors for books
feeding false truths to our youth,
teaching that hip hop hurts a generation
but it's not the pens
or the microphones doing the killing.
it's those stupid Europeans, making guns and graves
that's killing our children.
white bastards in suits
reading teleprompters
prompting and promoting me
to strangle your peter jennings looking ass.
God damn the media is like an abortion clinic
murdering my spirit.
telling us to strap on those Trojan like headphones
and protect ourselves from our culture,
like Jet Li
doesn't back flip and kick 36 dudes in each movie.
spiritually, you don't move me
but physically, you try to move me
from the tunes of classical rap music,
and Jadakiss is committing treason
speaking teachings about the George the Devil in the bushes
pushing our 18 year olds
into the deserts of death,
so i could spend
50 dollars on gas
rather,
give Ulysses S Grant to Akbar
while i drive to work every week
but don't speak on that,

sssssshhh!
let's close our eyes and look at how we show
up at the top of the hour every night,
from 10 til 12.
the fcc needs to put a cock, in larry king's ass
cause i'm tired of hearing his ignorant ass
cause the media is like an abortion clinic,
and i don't wanna be near it.
cause the problem solvers, ain't solving the problem
that our alert is Orange to Red at least once
every other month,
and we're still living in fear
and the more we know the less we're safe,
but did i thank barbara walters and the staff at 20/20
for showing me
lessons of decapitation,
because i'm sure that will come in handy
while i'm playing violent video games
on playstation 3 that's gonna
make me steal cars, and kill people,
like that shit can't already happen
in New York.
but we shouldn't worry because "Help is on the Way".
so, keep snapping pictures of Kerry and Edwards
cause they lost
without the gore shaft.
we can simply forget the constitution
and blame it on Jay Z for retiring,
and not telling us to vote,
while they keep blaming Columbines,
on combinations of music and movies.
let them point one finger (while three points back at them)
at the marilyn manson's, 50 cent's, and marshall mathers'
rather than,
dan rathers cause he's the real threat.
the media is like an abortion clinic,
and every night before
i go to sleep, i must watch
the devil's work tenfold,
over and over then wake up and read it
with my coffee, alright, read it with my shot of jack daniels
and listen to you tell me there's too much violence

in the songs,
in the lyrics,
in a spike lee joint,
in grand theft auto
but not the NEWS.
the current events, that sports stars are on trial,
that brothers and sisters
were sent off to be slaughtered
by Sadaams people because Bin Laden hit the towers ?
Wait,
By Sadaam's people, when Bin Laden, hit the towers?
and all of a sudden we forgot about Osama
cause cheaney has Getty and sunoco in his pocket
while vagina,
excuse me,
i mean bush holds amoco, exxon and mobil,
but we're supposed to be immobile
and listen to ted koppel
tell us that preachers and priests cop feels
off the youth,
and one of the greatest entertainers michael jackson,
which these same guys deem, "Wacko Jacko",
is home alone playing with Macaulay's culkin.
what is wrong with the media,
if anyone says a wrong word about that fat ass dead cokehead Elvis
Presley, the press is gonna press me,
then wanna press charges
and charge me with crimes to be splattered
all over TV and the radio, knifing me
scraping out my very insides,
scalpel...
and as i lay there, eyes bleeding to death
ears bleeding to deafness,
i'm trapped in that clinic, listening, entertaining myself
in the slandered bias views of society,
watching my culture
legs cocked in the air
spread eagle, stirrups clenching our flesh
ripping the very lives out of us...
the media y'all, is like an abortion clinic,
and if they say children are our future
we've gotta shut them down.

Catastrophes Definition

i sat there,
watching and listening.
i, society's acclaimed
sofa French fry,
while future fathers, mothers, poets,
were held hostage
by psychotic classmates,
destroying their lives
with pipe bombs. semi
automatic
murder addicts,
kill their peers with army tactics,
leaving all wondering if their safe or not,
being they hate people with hats, are black or jocks,
and while sane, scared students were second guessing
they asked questions,
"Do You Believe in Christ?"
bullet wounds that
decapitated and castrated,
left teens
unable to scream
while at simultaneous seconds, some
made their last hollers echo the hallway
like yells for help from those who excavate caves
and find bears
and left behind mutilated body parts
for family members
to identify
or keep for memorabilia
dreams of future graduates
departed
and started nightmares for parents
nightmares for many nights
of those who lived
after seeing
their best friend murdered and massacred
at the hands of
the guys nominated most likely to become serial killers
16 shots to the chest

and survivors struggle
teachers who gave "F's" escaped while those
who made sure
students passed,
passed...
grenade pins hit floors
as explosions knock down class doors
and as time runs out
windows blow out
and kids who want to live in wheelchairs
jump out,
rather don't wanna die fatally
leap for lady luck
parents reading lists
check to see
if they'll
only be cooking for the little ones tonight,
as the big ones, the future nightstick badge abusers
and Klansmen are
murdered by trench coat Nazi's
blowing out the candles
on Adolf's birthday cake
the youth has gotten so old,
so militant/ignorant,
both words being synonymous... the news showed views
of stretchers, I.V.'s and body bags
while the
devil had
a field day with his worshipers
they,
heads stricken with sickness
took peace
with their victims
while the media blames their parents rather than
blame themselves...
i still sat there,
watching and listening
to a documentary on Slavery.

History & Darkness

Six Hundred and Seventy Two hours.
Rather twenty eight days, to look back through the window
of history. A history
sang by Billie Holiday, while Louis Armstrong's horn,
and Lena Hornes voice,
caressed boiling blood,
that could not drink from that fountain.
We get, twenty eight days, to
sip the liquors of our heritage
while standing on the balcony
Kings passed on,
passing on the word of Nubian Queens
like the late greats of
Coretta, and Betty Shabazz,
and the pizzazz of
what we have, is embedded in
that melanin,
and i still smell the essence of home cooking.
Still felt the presence of home values,
and i value that tar like complexion
the mirror yells back to me.
Actually, i love the quiet celebrations of
slaves getting away, ssshhh!
Breaking the chains
and strains of our ancestry
which transcends from amendments to amnesty,
to graces amazingly,
to watching black athletes, and black congressmen, and
visions of blackness, and
the imminent sounds
of the percussions from the motherland.
That drumbeat, that heart beat, those rolling drums
beating while heartbeat's beat, skipped
from the smile
of our modern day Nefertiti.
The memories that enter me
when i ride the bus
sitting where i please
thanks to Rosa, thanks to my great great gran gran

who handed down
years of pain
for me to build a lifetime of triumph upon,
for us to walk proud,
heads held high
remembering them for more than twenty nine in a leap year,
but envelop their spirits within
our actions,
within the very thing which makes us who we are,
within our soul.
Soul. Soul clap, clapped and slapped the back of black men, rather niggers with
lips considered too big.
Lips, which spoke love to one another
in times of repression,
lips which uttered thoughts of escape from chains,
chaining a hatred past
to the chaining of a 'bruk' up structure called, a future with no peace,
but in pieces.
Yet, these so called pieces,
those so called twenty acres and a mule,
mule kicked a heritage lost
and forced us to a mere twenty eight.
twenty eight days, you give us to ram and cram a heritage buried
with dinosaur bones and fossils,
from the father,
with etched in negro spirituals in cracked skull,
full of the hope, dreams, and aspirations of
one. Just,
one soul.
Twenty eight million steps beyond
the imagination of Huey P. Newton.
Twenty eight synapses past,
Booker Ts and marching on Washington happenings,
and gatherings in and on Washington,
celebrating what you never wanted,
what we never dreamt,
while listing to King
speak speeches, leading us to Barack'ing the vote.
Having stepped out of the dark, gloomy shadows of nonexistent Hell,
rather ascend to heaven on Earth,
birthed by charcoal skin visions,

sending us spinning to whirlwinds of mother Africa,
realizations that unlocked,
we are stronger than the tides that bind us.
Now, with
pride set aside
from prejudices' injustice, and trust us the gist is,
the linguistics and logistics, that realities nightmare
ended from that balcony scene,
of that dreamers dream,
and our voices got louder,
love more defined,
the bleeding from the struggle
made our progression redefined.
Made the alphabets X quiet y and little z
and singing songs of wading in the water
by any means necessary.
The necessity of you, being there,
witnessing, yet listening
to voice of black goddess,
thoughts of young black king
re-rings the bell
and re-writes the captain's log on Amistad
un-understood,
misrepresented,
and overall bullshit but needed for him
to get where he got,
for us to get up and gather at polls to believe in the word Change,
to believe that we could pick up the shell of America and hear a voice like
ours
or steal that diamond studded mirror and witness
through red, white, and blue stripes. A face like ours,
facing the open cell Mandela walked out of,
embracing
the forty-one shots that revisited the nevers of reparations.
We are all on the court people.
From pretty boys to tar babies,
light skinned with good hair
to the dark and lovelies,
time is against us,
this is just day twenty four with only the fourth quarter to go,
but we've been on the bench so long
that now, getting into the game we couldn't watch,

we couldn't attend
or speak of (even in our inner most circles) is almost impossible.
They called it flat, but
it's Our World,
it's Our Destiny,
finally,
we're getting off the boat. My people,
we have ARRIVED.

Dim Bulbs, Highlighting a Year

September 8th, my birthday.
She, took a liking to the Isley brothers and got between the sheets with him.
There was no mistake in identity.
His skin, the color of the igloo built around my heart. His head, post chemo
as he inserts shaft within the cancer I've been injecting for the past three hundred and sixty six days.
She, leap years onto his frame,
one hundred and seventy eight pounds with a Photoshop, cropped physique.
She, rides him like the stallion she took her hair from,
in cheetah print bra,
while, ripped, dying cheetah print panties crawl to find peace, in a place to dry within his 13 inch Pumas.
October 31st she dresses as herself, the cheetah, tricking,
Rather the cheater, treating him to her chocolate.
He jollies in her rancher now,
And later she swallows his milky way as I'm galaxies away jacking my own lantern,
Carving my empty thoughts while he, digs out my pumpkin, his outfit reflects me,
Dark side, black cape, wielding that light saber just the way she loves it.
November 24th her cranberry sauce stains pant leg, and from stuffing her turkey,
She miscarried his candied yam, and I, am
Thankful.
Grateful that I won't feel the seed of his loin kick. and the soccer ball baby that could have been stays on her mind past December 25th,
As she was back to unwrapping his gifts of glory,
His ribbon secures her, and this ho ho ho still doesn't use paper, rubber, or any other contraceptive to prevent
His reindeer semen, from sliding down her chin, chimney like uterus
Or any other cavity he pops off the champagne top on January 1st,
New Year, same old shit.
February 14th I, slap a fat kid and shoot an arrow into Willy Wonkers ass.
I tell him what he's selling is for virgins, watching chick flicks hoping tonight's the night they've practiced putting condoms on since last
March 17th.
As she slept I whispered to her,

I heard his eyes were emeralds, traded for the lives of Irish men who couldn't handle their whiskey.
Whose women spread eagle for leprechauns with four leaf clovers tattooed on their testicles
Just to fuck lady luck back.
On April 1st,
She sent me a text message meant for him.
It spoke of springing all over one another as showers
Fall from the skies so they could use Gods rain to wash the filth of fornication off their
Sweaty, seductive, soul mate scented flesh
Like pornographic unicorns use waterfalls
while dragons watch, and masturbate from a distance like I did,
And I didn't say shit.
I just ignored her from Cinco de Mayo to the 4th of July
And prepared fireworks, steadied my nerves, brainwaves and my internal shot clock
as I readied for the violation, the flag, the whistle, the foot locker worker calling the play dead so I could march her ass
From the court, to the sideline to the locker room and I was fuming until August 23rd
When my stars aligned in the zodiac at a BBQ,
Between the bite of a piece of chicken and some collard greens
she screamed out she loved him.
She had given him all of her and kept nothing for me,
she said she waited for me to explode but all I did was write, and
What kind of man takes eyelids pinned to forehead to witness testicles snipped with dull, rusty scissors and then erupted by yelling
I never loved you!
I swallowed potato salad and spoke words calmer than waters Jesus stilled,
More at ease than tribes of babies lullabied by Dr. Seuss and Mother Goose reincarnated
with whispers of Negroes talking of Freedom,
And I said,
Listen garden tool, you, are a tear drop in the Atlantic,
A butterfly tattooed torso on a mummy, wrapped, encased and buried beneath lost cities in Egypt, no you are
a 10 watt light bulb in the center of a supernova,
a pebble amongst the fallen wall of Berlin,
The stench of wrapping human feces in human flesh and burning it on the stove top
With no fan, no windows, no doors.

No way to evacuate or ventilate the air you suck out of my diaphragm
forcing me to breathe thru mini straws served at the bar with cocktails,
And you're nothing more than a folk tale of sucking cock and giving your
tail away for free yet still owing men refunds.
The funny thing is cheetah girl,
my wife is pregnant, and due on your birthday.
Maybe that,
will make you relevant.

Friday Nights & DVRs

Ssssssssccccccuuuuurrrrrrr... BOOM!

10 minutes before the sweet sound of impact, I was,
both fists,
holding brain cells under brown paper bag.
Water, affixiating thoughts of cancer no, thoughts of love,
well drowning the equivocation of both.
Heart metastasizing,
while emotional data spreads all about anatomical structure.
Fallacy's lover,
touches her hand, touches her, like only a stranger would.
She couldn't like it!
But tonight, on the right side of my brain, she smiled,
meanwhile lymphocytes dodge radiations charger, and the Hemi tells me,
turn the ignition.

5 minutes before the serenity of the afterlife, breezed pass my windshield,
eyelids Kiel over,
from overdosing off optical vodka consumption.
My aorta's combustion,
pushes blood from chambers crushed, by alcohol's false testimony that
she'd, rather spend time away from the poet
who writes in chemo ink;
who bleeds words absent of white blood cells;
who thinks that pages make him walk on water like a God–
but I limp.
From lymph nodes mutating, rather, barely
hops,
cuz beer, turns brainwaves grizzly,
morphs heartbeat polar,
and as consciousness hibernates,
my limbs shake.
For a second, cerebellum is unsubmerged from the jealous rage of
Hennessy's radiation, and impact
further acts, as sobriety's alarm.
There is no snooze button on a tree in Queens,
no time like the present, to ignore her body, his wishes, or how thoughts of
the two become one like PB&J in my minds cell,
or how cells within, imprison me, cutting–
the edges off my life.

LAUNDROMATS & LOUNGES

The knife inside holds no fingerprints different than
paper mate which scripts lyrics of liquor,
bottle empty of toxins consumed,
serving as swimming pool for all which weighs on cerebrum,
to cannonball with four wheels thru a pole, into nothing
but a failed suicide attempt.

Half Cracked, Fully Shattered

Wrapped in the comfort
of nightmares, sin and a quilt of
my short comings and inequity, i
laid my head on the firm
pillowcase of armadillo, covering
the pillow stuffed of ostrich feathers
and porcupine quills.
The sheets, gave off a stench of 70 hour work weeks, intertwined
with alcoholics ruminate,
and sickening sessions of self rape, but
they seemed to emasculate
the mattress made of pumice.
Something lying still just ready to erupt.
The walls were painted in a disrupted intestinal color and the asbestos
steadily fell from the ceiling,
like the nor'easter outside the windows. Windows half cracked, fully
shattered.
Zero visibility and they allowed
the very core, of warmth out of the room.
The blinds are dingy. They conceal misery, and seldom does light shine in.
The door, off the hinges. Perfect outlet
for constant confusion and no separation from the rest of what one might
consider home.
The ground. Quarter concrete. Quarter-stained carpet from late night
coffee, over indulged chocolate snacks, kerosene, smeared lipstick and
blotches of semen; quarter hardwood, and a quarter missing, endorsing my
vision to clichés of boiler room basements.
The furniture, brand new, termite infested charcoal gray chopping wood
fresh from a man with no
future, no hopes, no past worth trying
to fight brain cells to remember,
a man who I'm becoming. And
this, only one week after you moved out, with heart,
half cracked, fully shattered.

Emocean (ih-moh-shuhn)

It begins with great hope, the fluttering
of one's heart in anticipation
of that four letter word,
scam
of what daddy said it would feel
like getting swept off your feet
under the Eiffel Tower by a Swedish model
in a French maid's dress,
yet you vividly hear a Créole accent. Take in as
much oxygen as she will allow you before you enter her,
recollections of every word uttered
as gravity pulls you into those deep,
blue...
she is colder than you imagined,
rough and brutal throwing you around
like a bouncer does a drunkard long after last call,
hours after happy hour.
Seconds into the last minutes you gasp,
forgetting she's all around, like the Savior a Christian
would try to scream for. Manhood
dwindles as she gorges the branches of bronchi,
eyes water but merely build her mass.
Climax calms, as does all movement.
Sssshhhh she whispers,
be still,
and float on top of me.

Transcendence

In the moment, of the moment,
I kissed the darkness.

Her mouth, let light shine through blinds crazy glued, and drapes,
stapled by bloody, tetanus infested
staples were nailed to the windows pane,
while the Lord's tears, shimmied down
cracked glass.

Gabriel, packed suitcase for me
though his hands didn't move.
Motionless motives, manage to try and prepare me for my most awaited
voyage.

He whispers Exodus, i hear, Diaspora.

All of life is a well lit room, if you're in it, there's bound to be a shadow.

Etches of Life's Tomb

they're gonna bury me a poet.
they're gonna speak of soothing quotations
wrapped around letters,
like envelops enveloping
a spirit. A spirit
that whispered dreams of getting closer to the holy spirit.
they're gonna bury me a man.
a man, whose hands
beat on eardrums while
caressing microphones, souls, and women
who fall in love with,
verbal bloodshed from the epitome
of things i strive to be,
because of the essence, of reminiscence on Calvary.
they're gonna bury me a father.
whose offspring,
sprung off genius, diva, musician, artist
and helped mold creativity in the rarest
form of innocence,
and created a protection from the serpent, by arming them
with scriptures inspired by the word of
my creator.
they're gonna bury me a son.
a shining star/descendant of Moses, parting the seas
allowing all to see the inner me, the inside where He dwells.
a son begotten by mother and father,
who melted their experiences into a distinctive ink,
and scribed strong stern
illustrations of passion, intimacy, stability
and how to envision the value of vows.
they're gonna bury me a husband.
who focuses on maintaining
the synchronization of every single beat, of our hearts.
who keeps every emotion she shares,
master locked within
the fist size structure, pumping, in my chest cavity.
they're gonna bury me a brother.
sibling unrivaled in the arena of global reassurance,
anything he needs

that can be offered, consider it done, like Peter would to Paul would to Mark
back to Matthew, Andrew and John.
washing the sorrows of his brothers away, keeping them
as keeper would, as intended by terms of endearment,
teammates on the greatest team assembled.
they're gonna bury me a friend.
who supplies Kleenex sweaters
covering ready-access to lean on shoulders,
and auditory canals willing to listen
when the rest of the Earth is stricken with the deaf plague.
they're gonna bury me,
and chat bout artist, black nationalist, hard worker,
free spirit, cancer survivor, college graduate, catalyst for much clown activity,
but before they bury me
i just want you to know, that i lived
as His vessel.

ABOUT THE AUTHOR

Born in Brooklyn, New York of Bajan descent, Roger Smith struggled through his teens and twenties with considering himself as a poet. With thoughts of the cliché that poetry "doesn't put food on the table", he switched majors and directions continuously during his early years as an undergraduate, until finally declaring himself an English major at Molloy College where he will graduate with a BA in English in 2014. Married for 11 years with three daughters, Smith, a baptized member of the Seventh Day Adventist Church, scribes with an intense personal voice and illustrates poetry that generates instant images to his readers, inspirational thoughts of love, yet still deals with the ugly truths of reality. His poetry has been published in the Molloy College Literary Magazine, and he has performed at various venues in New York City and plans on continuing to share his gift with the world through being what God has made him, a poet.

ROGER SMITH

Made in the USA
Lexington, KY
10 May 2013